Welcome to "Quick and Easy Low Budget Lunch Recipes" cookbook, where we have gathered a collection of delicious, healthy and affordable lunch recipes to make your life easier.

We understand the struggle of having a busy schedule and trying to maintain a balanced diet on a tight budget. That's why we've created this cookbook to provide you with simple, yet tasty lunch options that won't break the bank.

Inside, you'll find a variety of recipes that are easy to prepare and don't require fancy ingredients or equipment. From sandwiches, salads, soups, and wraps to pasta dishes, stir-fries, and more, there's something for everyone.

Whether you're a student, a busy professional, or just looking for some new lunch ideas, this cookbook has got you covered. So, grab your apron and get ready to cook up some delicious and affordable lunches that you'll love!

Grilled Chicken Kebab

Ingredients:

1 pound boneless, skinless chicken breasts, cut into 1-inch cubes
1/4 cup olive oil
2 tablespoons fresh lemon juice
2 cloves garlic, minced
1 teaspoon paprika
1 teaspoon ground cumin
1/2 teaspoon salt
1/4 teaspoon black pepper
Wooden or metal skewers
Optional: diced onion, bell pepper, and/or cherry tomatoes for skewering

Instructions:

If using wooden skewers, soak them in water for at least 30 minutes to prevent burning during grilling.
In a small bowl, whisk together the olive oil, lemon juice, garlic, paprika, cumin, salt, and black pepper.
Place the chicken cubes in a large zip-top bag and pour the marinade over the top. Seal the bag and refrigerate for at least 1 hour (or up to 8 hours) to allow the flavors to penetrate the meat.
Preheat a grill to medium-high heat.
If using vegetables, thread them onto skewers along with the marinated chicken cubes.
Grill the chicken kebabs for 10-12 minutes, turning occasionally, until the chicken is cooked through and slightly charred on the outside.
Serve hot, garnished with fresh herbs and a squeeze of lemon juice, if desired. Enjoy!

Cacio e Pepe

Ingredients:

8 ounces spaghetti or other long pasta
1 cup grated Pecorino Romano cheese
1 teaspoon freshly ground black pepper
Salt
2 tablespoons unsalted butter

Instructions:

Cook the spaghetti in a large pot of boiling salted water according to the package instructions until al dente.
While the spaghetti is cooking, in a large skillet, melt the butter over medium heat.
Add the black pepper and toast it for a minute or so until fragrant.
Using a ladle, scoop out about 1 cup of the pasta cooking water and set it aside.
Drain the spaghetti and add it to the skillet with the pepper and butter.
Toss the spaghetti with the pepper and butter until coated.
Remove the skillet from the heat and sprinkle the grated Pecorino Romano cheese over the spaghetti.
Add a splash or two of the reserved pasta cooking water and toss the spaghetti again until the cheese is melted and the sauce is creamy.
If the sauce is too thick, add more of the reserved pasta cooking water until you reach the desired consistency.
Taste and adjust the seasoning with salt, if necessary.
Serve the cacio e pepe hot, garnished with additional grated Pecorino Romano cheese and black pepper. Enjoy!

Chicken Fried Rice

Chicken Fried Rice is a delicious, easy and fast meal that you can prepare in minutes. It's one of the most popular chicken recipes around, and it's easy to see why! This comfort food dish packs plenty of flavor and nutrition all into one easy-to-make meal.

The ingredients in Chicken Fried Rice are simple, but the flavors are anything but. Start by heating oil (both sesame and vegetable) in a wok or large skillet over medium-high heat. Once hot, add chicken breasts and sauté until cooked through. Add frozen peas and carrots, green onions, garlic, eggs and cooked rice to the pan and cook until everything is heated through. Finally, stir in low-sodium soy sauce for some added flavor and serve.

With just a few simple ingredients and easy steps, you can have a delicious meal ready to go in no time! So next time you're looking for an easy and flavorful chicken recipe, give Chicken Fried Rice a try - it's sure to be a hit!

Happy cooking!

Baked Potato Bar

Ingredients

5 pounds baked potatoes.
3-5 pounds pulled pork cooked.
2 cups sharp cheddar cheese shredded.
1/2 pound bacon cooked & crumbled.
1 cup sour cream.
1/2 cup chives chopped.
2 cups broccoli cooked.
1 bottle bbq sauce.

A baked potato bar is an easy and healthy dinner option for kids, and it's simple to prepare. Start by baking five pounds of potatoes according to the instructions on the package. While they're cooking, pre-cook three to five pounds of pulled pork as well as one-half pound of bacon. Once the potatoes are done, split them open and sprinkle two cups of shredded sharp cheddar cheese over the top. Then, add the cooked pulled pork, crumbled bacon, one cup of sour cream, half a cup of chopped chives and two cups of cooked broccoli. Finally, make sure to provide some BBQ sauce for everyone to enjoy. With minimal effort, you can create a delicious and nutritious baked potato bar that all the kids will love! Enjoy!

Baked Feta Pasta

ingredients

2 pints (20 oz) grape tomatoes.
1/2 cup extra-virgin olive oil.
Salt and freshly ground black pepper.
7 oz. block feta cheese (sheep's milk variety), drained.
10 oz. dry pasta (bite size)
5 medium garlic cloves, peeled and halved.
8 oz. ...
1/4 tsp crushed red pepper flakes, or more to taste.

Baked Feta Pasta is an easy and healthy dish that takes only minimal time to prepare. With just a handful of simple ingredients, you can create this delicious meal. To make it, start by preheating your oven to 425 degrees Fahrenheit.

In a large bowl, combine the grape tomatoes, extra-virgin olive oil, salt and pepper. Cut the feta cheese into small cubes and add it to the bowl. Next, cook 10 oz of bite-size pasta according to package instructions until al dente. Once done, drain it and mix it with the tomato mixture in the bowl.

Add garlic cloves, 8 oz of mushrooms (sliced), and 1/4 tsp of crushed red pepper flakes, or to taste. Toss everything together and spread it in a single layer on an oven-safe dish. Bake for 25 minutes until the top is lightly golden brown.

Baked Feta Pasta is now ready to enjoy! Serve with a sprinkling of fresh herbs, extra olive oil, and a side of crusty bread. This healthy pasta dish makes for a great weeknight dinner that is sure to please the whole family. Enjoy!

Best Grilled Chicken Breast

Ingredients:

4 boneless, skinless chicken breasts
1/4 cup olive oil
2 tablespoons lemon juice
2 cloves garlic, minced
1 teaspoon dried thyme
1 teaspoon dried rosemary
1/2 teaspoon salt
1/4 teaspoon black pepper

Instructions:

Preheat your grill to medium-high heat.
In a small bowl, whisk together olive oil, lemon juice, minced garlic, dried thyme, dried rosemary, salt, and black pepper.
Place the chicken breasts in a shallow dish or large resealable bag. Pour the marinade over the chicken and toss to coat. Let the chicken marinate for at least 30 minutes, or up to 4 hours in the refrigerator.
Once the grill is hot, remove the chicken from the marinade and discard any remaining marinade.
Place the chicken breasts on the grill and cook for about 5-6 minutes per side, or until the internal temperature of the chicken reaches 165°F (75°C) on an instant-read thermometer.
Once the chicken is cooked through, remove it from the grill and let it rest for a few minutes before serving.
Serve the grilled chicken breasts with your favorite sides and enjoy!
Note: For best results, make sure to let the chicken come to room temperature for 15-20 minutes before grilling, and make sure to oil the grill grates before cooking to prevent sticking.

Chicken Quesadillas

Ingredients

1 pound skinless, boneless chicken breast, diced.
1 (1.27 ounce) packet fajita seasoning.
1 tablespoon vegetable oil.
2 green bell peppers, chopped.
2 red bell peppers, chopped.
1 onion, chopped. ...
10 (10 inch) flour tortillas.
1 (8 ounce) package shredded Cheddar cheese.

Chicken quesadillas make for a healthy and easy dinner for the whole family. To start preparing, dice the boneless chicken breasts and season with fajita seasoning. In a large skillet over medium heat, heat vegetable oil and add in the diced chicken breast, green bell peppers, red bell peppers, and onions. Cook until vegetables are softened and chicken is cooked through. To assemble the quesadillas, place about ¼ cup of cheese onto one side of a tortilla. Top with cooked vegetables and chicken, then add another ¼ cup of cheese to the top. Fold over into a half-moon shape and cook in a skillet on medium-high heat until golden brown. Repeat this process with the remaining tortillas. Serve warm and enjoy!

For a fun variation, try adding black beans to the quesadillas or swapping out Cheddar cheese for Monterey Jack. Using flavorful ingredients like jalapenos, salsa, and guacamole can also liven up this classic dish. Chicken quesadillas make for a healthy and delicious dinner that can be customized to fit the tastes of any family. Enjoy!

Spaghetti Alla Putanesca

Ingredients

400 grams of spaghetti
100 grams of pitted olives
1 tablespoon salted capers
500 grams of well-ripened tomatoes or 400 grams of tomatoes in broth
2 large garlic cloves
5-6 anchovy fillets salted or in oil
1 sprig parsley
3-4 tablespoons olive oil
salt and pepper
optional: chilli pepper, fresh or dried

If you're looking for delicious recipes for kids, look no further than spaghetti alla Puttanesca. This classic Italian dish is easy to make and packed with flavour. Here's how to cook it:

Firstly, bring a large pot of salted water to a rolling boil and add the 400 grams of spaghetti. Cook until al dente, then strain and set aside.

In a large skillet over medium heat, add the 3-4 tablespoons of olive oil and two large cloves of garlic, chopped. When the garlic begins to sizzle, stir for about 30 seconds before adding anchovy fillets salted or in oil. Stir until the anchovies have dissolved into the oil.

Now you can add the pitted olives and capers, stirring for another 1-2 minutes before adding 500 grams of well-ripened tomatoes or 400 grams of tomatoes in broth. Season with salt and pepper to taste, plus chilli pepper if desired. Simmer for about 10 minutes until all the flavours have combined.

Finally, add the strained spaghetti and stir for 1-2 minutes to ensure everything is well mixed together. Serve in bowls with freshly chopped parsley as a garnish. Enjoy!

Chicken Noodle Casserole

Ingredients
12 oz. wide egg noodles.
10.5-oz. cans cream of chicken soup.
1 c. whole milk.
1 c. shredded sharp cheddar cheese.
1 tsp. ground black pepper.
1/2 tsp. kosher salt.
3 c. cooked, shredded chicken (from 1 rotisserie chicken)
1/2. small yellow onion, finely chopped.

Making a chicken noodle casserole is an easy and healthy dinner option for kids. To begin, preheat your oven to 400 degrees Fahrenheit. In a large pot over medium heat, cook the egg noodles according to package directions. Drain the cooked noodles and set aside.

In a medium-sized bowl, combine the cream of chicken soup, milk, shredded cheese, ground black pepper and kosher salt. Stir until the ingredients are completely blended.

In a 9-by-13-inch baking dish, spread the cooked egg noodles. Top with the shredded chicken and onion pieces. Pour the cream of chicken mixture over the noodles and chicken, spreading evenly to ensure everything is coated.

Bake for 25 minutes until the cheese is melted and bubbly. Let cool for about 10 minutes before serving. Enjoy!

This chicken noodle casserole provides a comforting, delicious and healthy dinner option for kids. It's quick to prepare, full of flavor and sure to please everyone at the table.

Spinach And Feta Pizza

Ingredients

2 large Pizza Bases (see notes)
½ cup Tomato Paste.
½ Brown / Yellow Onion, finely diced.
½ Red Capsicum / Bell Pepper, finely diced.
100g / 3.5 oz Baby Spinach, roughly chopped.
4 White Mushrooms, thinly sliced.
½ cup Feta Cheese, crumbled.
1 ½ cups Shredded Mozzarella Cheese (or more, to taste)

Making delicious spinach and feta pizzas is easy and delicious. To begin, preheat your oven to 200°C / 392°F. Place the pizza bases on a lightly greased baking tray. Spread a thin layer of tomato paste over each base, then scatter the diced onion, capsicum / bell pepper, mushrooms, baby spinach and crumbled feta cheese over the top. Sprinkle with mozzarella cheese (you can add more if desired). Bake for 15-20 minutes or until golden brown and bubbly. Serve hot! Enjoy your delicious spinach and feta pizza!

These delicious spinach and feta pizzas are sure to become a family favorite in no time! The combination of flavors from the vegetables, feta and mozzarella cheese makes for a delicious meal that is sure to please everyone. With just a few simple ingredients, you can easily make delicious pizza recipes at home with ease! No need to order take-out anymore - now you can make delicious pizzas right in your own kitchen. Enjoy!

Grilled Hot Dogs

Grilled hot dogs are a classic summer cookout favorite. They're also an easy and healthy dinner option for kids. Preparing grilled hot dogs is super simple - all you need to do is gather the ingredients, heat up your grill, and get cooking!

To prepare grilled hot dogs, you'll need eight hot dogs, ¼ cup ketchup, 2 Tbsp Worcestershire Sauce, 1 minced garlic clove, and 1 tsp of vegetable oil. Start by preheating the grill to medium-high heat. Once it's hot enough, place the hot dogs on the grill and cook for about 8 minutes or until browned and cooked through.

In a small bowl, mix together the ketchup, Worcestershire sauce, garlic and vegetable oil. Brush the hot dogs with the mixture when they come off of the grill. Serve with your favorite condiments and sides for a delicious summer meal! Enjoy!

Chicken Tacos

Ingredients

¼ cup olive oil.
2 medium yellow onions, finely chopped.
2 bell peppers (any color), finely chopped.
4 cloves garlic, finely chopped.
2 pounds ground chicken (not extra-lean all breast meat)
1 tablespoon paprika.
2 teaspoons ancho chili powder.
1½ teaspoons ground cumin.

Preparing chicken tacos is a healthy and easy dinner option that kids will love. To make them, begin by heating ¼ cup of olive oil in a large skillet over medium-high heat. Add in chopped onions and bell peppers, as well as the minced garlic, stirring everything until it's lightly browned and fragrant.
Then, add in the ground chicken, breaking it up with a spoon as you stir. Once the chicken is cooked through, sprinkle in paprika, ancho chili powder and cumin. Stir everything to combine and let it cook for 3-4 minutes until all of the flavors have melded together.
Once done, serve your chicken tacos with tortillas, your favorite toppings and a side dish. Enjoy!

This is an easy yet tasty way to whip up a healthy dinner for the kids! By following these easy steps, you can have a delicious batch of chicken tacos ready in no time. Not only are they healthy and delicious, but your kids will love them too! Try it out today for a quick and tasty dinner option.

Enjoy!

Tofu Sandwich

Are you looking for vegetarian recipes for kids? Then look no further than this delicious tofu sandwich. It's a healthy and easy meal that your children will adore. Start by toasting some of their favorite bread, and spread with Thousand Island dressing. To make the sandwich extra special, add lettuce, tomatoes, avocado, cucumber and sprouts. This vegetarian recipe is sure to please everyone in the family! To prepare it, simply assemble all of the ingredients into the sandwich and serve. Your kids will love it! Enjoy!

The tofu sandwich is a great vegetarian alternative for kids and makes a healthy, easy meal that can be prepared quickly. A delicious combination of toasted bread, Thousand Island dressing, lettuce, tomatoes, avocado, cucumber and sprouts makes this vegetarian recipe both nutritious and tasty. It's an ideal way to get your kids to enjoy vegetarian meals - just assemble the ingredients into the sandwich and serve! Your children will love it and you can feel good knowing they are getting their daily dose of veggies. Kids need all the nutrition they can get - so why not try this vegetarian recipe today? Enjoy!

Carbonara Spaghetti

Carbonara spaghetti is a delicious recipe for kids to learn how to cook. The ingredients you will need are 100g of pancetta, 50g of pecorino cheese, 50g of parmesan, 3 large eggs, 350g of spaghetti, 2 plump garlic cloves (peeled and left whole), 50g unsalted butter, sea salt, and freshly ground black pepper. To begin cooking this delicious dish, bring a large saucepan of salted water to the boil. Add the spaghetti and cook until al dente (around 8-10 minutes). Meanwhile, fry the pancetta in a dry non-stick frying pan over moderate heat for about 5 minutes until lightly golden. Once cooked, set aside and keep warm. In a small bowl, mix together the pecorino cheese and parmesan with the eggs until you have a creamy sauce. Season well with salt and pepper. When the spaghetti is cooked, drain it, reserving some of the cooking water. Add the spaghetti to the pan with the pancetta and garlic, and stir everything together. Add the butter, stirring until melted. Pour over the egg mixture and toss everything together well with a little of the reserved cooking water - this will help to make it nice and creamy. Serve immediately while still warm. Enjoy!

This delicious carbonara spaghetti dish is sure to be a hit with the whole family. With just a few ingredients and simple steps, your kids can learn to make this delicious dinner in no time! Serve it with a fresh salad on the side for a delicious meal that everyone will love. Enjoy!

Grilled Potatoes

Ingredients:

1 1/2 pounds baby potatoes (or small Yukon gold or red potatoes), halved
2 tablespoons olive oil
1 tablespoon chopped fresh rosemary
1 tablespoon chopped fresh thyme
1/2 teaspoon garlic powder
Salt and black pepper, to taste

Instructions:

Preheat your grill to medium-high heat.
In a large bowl, combine halved potatoes, olive oil, chopped rosemary, chopped thyme, garlic powder, salt, and black pepper. Toss to coat evenly.
Cut a sheet of aluminum foil, about 18 inches long. Place the seasoned potatoes on the center of the foil sheet.
Fold the foil over the potatoes and seal the edges tightly to create a packet.
Place the foil packet on the grill and cook for about 20-25 minutes, or until the potatoes are tender when pierced with a fork. Flip the packet halfway through cooking to ensure even cooking.
Once the potatoes are done, carefully open the foil packet and transfer the potatoes to a serving dish. Serve immediately and enjoy!
Note: You can also add sliced onions, bell peppers or mushrooms to the packet to add some extra flavor and texture. And if you prefer crispy potatoes, you can grill them without the foil directly on the grates, but make sure to keep an eye on them as they can burn easily.

Easy Frittata

Ingredients:

6 large eggs
1/4 cup milk or heavy cream
1/2 teaspoon salt
1/4 teaspoon black pepper
2 tablespoons olive oil
1 small onion, chopped
1 small bell pepper, chopped
1 cup chopped cooked ham, bacon, or sausage
1 cup shredded cheese (cheddar, mozzarella, or your favorite)
Fresh herbs for garnish (optional)

Instructions:

Preheat the oven to 350°F (175°C).

In a large mixing bowl, whisk together the eggs, milk or heavy cream, salt, and black pepper.
Heat the olive oil in a 10-inch oven-safe skillet over medium heat.
Add the chopped onion and bell pepper to the skillet and cook until softened, about 5-7 minutes.
Add the chopped ham, bacon, or sausage to the skillet and cook for another 2-3 minutes until heated through.
Pour the egg mixture into the skillet, and sprinkle the shredded cheese on top.
Gently stir the ingredients with a spatula to distribute the filling evenly in the skillet.
Transfer the skillet to the preheated oven and bake for 15-20 minutes until the frittata is set and the cheese is melted and bubbly.
Remove the skillet from the oven and let it cool for a few minutes.
Use a spatula to slide the frittata onto a large plate. Garnish with fresh herbs, if desired.
Slice the frittata into wedges and serve warm or at room temperature. Enjoy!

Lemon Mushroom Chicken

Ingredients:

4 chicken breasts (about 3/4 pound total)
1 1/2 tbsp unsalted butter, divided
8 oz cremini mushrooms, sliced
1/4 tsp salt
1/2 cup dry sherry
1/4 cup lemon juice
1/2 cup heavy cream
2 1/2 cups baby spinach

Instructions:

Season the chicken breasts with salt and pepper.

In a large pan, heat 1 tbsp of butter over medium heat. Add the chicken breasts and cook for about 4-5 minutes on each side, or until golden brown and fully cooked. Remove the chicken from the pan and set aside.

In the same pan, add the remaining butter and sliced mushrooms. Cook the mushrooms for about 4-5 minutes, or until they are tender and lightly browned.

Add the sherry to the pan and use a wooden spoon to scrape the bottom of the pan to release any browned bits. Cook the sherry for about 2 minutes, or until it has reduced by half.

Add the lemon juice and heavy cream to the pan and stir to combine. Cook the sauce for about 2-3 minutes, or until it has thickened slightly.

Return the chicken breasts to the pan and add the baby spinach. Stir to combine and cook for about 2 minutes, or until the spinach has wilted.

Serve the chicken with the lemon mushroom sauce on top. Enjoy!

Pasta alla Norma

Ingredients:

1 lb spaghetti
1 large eggplant, diced
2 cloves garlic, minced
1 can (28 oz) whole peeled tomatoes, crushed by hand
1/4 teaspoon red pepper flakes
Salt and pepper to taste
1/4 cup chopped fresh basil
1/2 cup grated ricotta salata cheese
Extra-virgin olive oil

Instructions:

Bring a large pot of salted water to a boil. Add the spaghetti and cook according to package instructions until al dente.

While the spaghetti cooks, heat a large skillet over medium-high heat. Add enough olive oil to coat the bottom of the pan.
Add the diced eggplant to the skillet and cook for about 8-10 minutes, or until the eggplant is golden brown and tender.
Add the minced garlic and red pepper flakes to the skillet and cook for another minute, or until fragrant.
Add the crushed tomatoes to the skillet and season with salt and pepper to taste.
Simmer the sauce for about 10-15 minutes, or until it has thickened slightly.
Drain the cooked spaghetti and add it to the skillet with the tomato sauce. Toss to combine.
Remove the skillet from the heat and stir in the chopped basil.
Divide the pasta among four bowls and sprinkle each serving with grated ricotta salata cheese.
Enjoy your delicious Pasta alla Norma!

Chicken And Creamy Bacon Penne

Ingredients

1 tbsp olive oil.
2 boneless skinless chicken breasts.
100g smoked lardon (chopped bacon)
4 tbsp dry white wine.
100g frozen petits pois.
5 tbsp double cream.
8220g packet cooked penne.!

Chicken with creamy bacon penne is a delicious recipe for kids that's easy to cook. Begin by heating the olive oil in a large non-stick pan and adding the chicken breasts. Cook these until golden brown, then add the chopped lardon (bacon) and fry until crisp. Next, pour in the white wine, stirring continuously to prevent sticking. Once the wine has reduced by half, add in small handfuls of frozen petits pois and stir until cooked through.

Finally, reduce to a low heat and add in the double cream and cooked penne. Stir continuously for 4-5 minutes until all ingredients are combined and creamy sauce is formed. Serve hot for delicious family meal. Enjoy!

Avocado Fusilli Pasta

Ingredients

350g fusilli.
2 cloves garlic, peeled.
200g baby spinach.
2 small ripe avocados, halved and stoned.
extra-virgin olive oil, for drizzling.
30g roasted cashews, chopped.
30g roasted almonds, chopped.
a small bunch coriander, chopped.

For healthy and delicious pasta, you can't go wrong with this avocado fusilli recipe! Start by bringing a large pot of salted water to the boil. Add the fusilli and cook until al dente. Meanwhile, in a large pan over medium heat, add some olive oil and garlic cloves. Saute for 5 minutes until fragrant. Add the baby spinach and cook for a few minutes until wilted. When the pasta is cooked, drain it and add to the pan with the spinach mixture. Finally, top with halved avocados, roasted cashews and almonds and chopped coriander. Drizzle with some extra-virgin olive oil for a healthy finish. Serve and enjoy! This healthy pasta dish is sure to become a favorite in your house. With its creamy avocado, crunchy nuts, and delicious flavors from the garlic, spinach and coriander, it's an easy healthy meal that everyone can enjoy. Try this avocado fusilli recipe today!

Risotto

Ingredients:

1 1/2 cups Arborio or Carnaroli rice
4 cups chicken or vegetable broth
1/2 cup dry white wine
1/4 cup unsalted butter
1/2 cup grated Parmesan cheese
1 onion, finely chopped
2 garlic cloves, minced
2 tablespoons olive oil
Salt and freshly ground black pepper
Optional ingredients: mushrooms, asparagus, peas, shrimp, chicken, or any other vegetables or proteins you'd like to add

Instructions:

In a large saucepan, heat the broth over medium heat until it's simmering.
In a separate large pot, heat the olive oil over medium heat. Add the chopped onion and minced garlic and sauté until the onion is translucent, about 5 minutes.
Add the Arborio rice to the pot and stir to coat the rice in the oil, onion, and garlic mixture.
Add the white wine and stir continuously until it has been absorbed by the rice.
Begin adding the simmering broth to the pot, one cup at a time, stirring constantly until each cup of broth has been absorbed by the rice before adding the next.
Continue adding broth and stirring until the rice is tender and creamy. This process should take about 20-25 minutes.
When the rice is done, stir in the grated Parmesan cheese and season with salt and pepper to taste.
Serve immediately and enjoy!

Chicken Noodle Soup

Ingredients
2 tablespoons unsalted butter.
1 onion, diced.
2 carrots, peeled and diced.
2 celery ribs, diced.
3 cloves garlic, minced.
8 cups chicken stock.
2 bay leaves.
Kosher salt freshly ground black pepper, to taste.

Chicken noodle soup is a delicious, healthy and easy dinner option for kids. To prepare it, start by melting the butter over medium heat in a large pot. Add the onion, carrots and celery to the pot and cook until softened, about 5 minutes. Stir in garlic until fragrant, about 1 minute. Pour in chicken stock, bay leaves, salt and pepper. Bring the soup to a boil. Reduce heat and simmer for 15 minutes or until the vegetables are tender. Finally, add noodles and cook according to package instructions. Serve hot with your favorite toppings such as shredded cheese, croutons or chopped parsley. Enjoy!

Greek Pasta Salad

Greek Pasta Salad is a vegetarian recipe that can be enjoyed by kids and adults alike. It's a healthy, vibrant dish with plenty of flavor to keep everyone happy! To make this delicious salad, start by boiling 12 ounces of mini farfalle pasta according to package instructions. Drain and set aside to cool. While the pasta is cooling, prepare the other ingredients: halve and pit 1/2 cup Kalamata olives; dice 1/3 cup red onion; cut 2 cups English or Persian cucumbers into half moons; halve 2 cups (1 pint) cherry tomatoes; dice 1 cup green bell pepper; chop 1/4 cup parsley; cube 1/2 cup feta cheese.

Once all the ingredients are ready, combine them in a large bowl. Add the cooled pasta, olives, red onion, cucumbers, tomatoes, bell pepper, parsley and feta cheese. Mix everything together until evenly combined. Serve chilled or at room temperature. Enjoy!

This vegetarian recipe is sure to be a hit with your kids. Not only is it healthy and full of flavor but it's also easy to make. You can prepare all the components ahead of time and let everyone customize their own bowl with their favorite ingredients. Greek Pasta Salad is perfect for lunchboxes or as part of a special weekend meal. Bon appétit!

Bolognese Spaghetti

Ingredients
1 tbsp olive oil.
4 rashers smoked streaky bacon, finely chopped.
2 medium onions, finely chopped.
2 carrots, trimmed and finely chopped.
2 celery sticks, finely chopped.
2 garlic cloves finely chopped.
2-3 sprigs rosemary leaves picked and finely chopped.
500g beef mince.

If you're looking for delicious recipes for kids, look no further than bolognese spaghetti! This classic Italian pasta dish is packed with flavour and can be made in no time. Plus, children of all ages will love it! Here's how to cook the perfect bolognese spaghetti:

Begin by heating 1 tablespoon of olive oil in a large frying pan. Add 4 finely chopped rashers of smoked streaky bacon, 2 finely chopped onions, 2 trimmed and finely chopped carrots, 2 finely chopped celery sticks, 2 finely chopped garlic cloves and the leaves from 2-3 sprigs of rosemary that have been picked and finely chopped. Cook the ingredients until the bacon and vegetables are softened.

Next, add 500g of beef mince to the pan and season with salt and pepper. Stir everything together and cook for about 10 minutes until the mince is browned. Finally, pour in a jar or can of tomato sauce or passata, along with a little water if necessary. Simmer for 10 minutes, then serve over cooked hot spaghetti.

Your delicious bolognese spaghetti dish is now ready to be enjoyed. Add a sprinkle of grated cheese and a dash of chilli flakes if desired. Bon appétit!

Pineapple Chicken Casserole

Here's a list of ingredients for a pineapple chicken casserole:

2 cups cubed cooked chicken
1 can (10-1/2 ounces) condensed cream of mushroom soup
1 cup pineapple tidbits
2 celery ribs, chopped
1 tablespoon chopped green onion
1 tablespoon reduced-sodium soy sauce
1 can (3 ounces) chow mein noodles, divided

Instructions:

Preheat the oven to 350°F (175°C).

In a large bowl, combine the chicken, cream of mushroom soup, pineapple tidbits, chopped celery, green onion, and soy sauce.

Pour the mixture into a 2-quart baking dish.

Crush half of the chow mein noodles and sprinkle them over the top of the chicken mixture.

Bake the casserole in the preheated oven for 30 minutes, or until heated through and the top is golden and crispy.

Serve the casserole hot, garnished with the remaining chow mein noodles and additional chopped green onion, if desired. Enjoy!

Cheesy Broccoli Pasta

Ingredients
½ cup butter.
1 onion, chopped. Fresh Onions.
1 (16 ounce) package frozen chopped broccoli.
4 (14.5 ounce) cans chicken broth.
1 (1 pound) loaf processed cheese food, cubed.
2 cups milk.
1 tablespoon garlic powder.
⅔ cup cornstarch.

This delicious cheesy broccoli pasta is a sure hit for kids and adults alike! With just a few simple steps, anyone can make this delicious dish in no time.

First, melt the butter in a large pot over medium heat. Add the chopped onion and cook until softened, about 5 minutes. Next, add the frozen chopped broccoli and chicken broth and bring to a boil. Reduce the heat, cover, and simmer for 15 minutes.

Once done, add the cubed cheese food, milk, garlic powder and cornstarch to the pot. Give it all a good stir then cover and cook for about 10 more minutes or until the sauce has thickened. Serve hot with your favorite sides!

This cheesy broccoli pasta is delicious and easy to make, making it an ideal recipe for kids. If you're looking for a delicious and nutritious dish that your whole family can enjoy, this is the perfect choice! So what are you waiting for? Try out this delicious cheesy broccoli pasta today!

Enjoy

Tuna Pasta

Ingredients

2 tablespoons olive oil.
2 large cloves garlic minced.
1 (5 ounce) can tuna, drained I prefer tuna packed in oil.
1 teaspoon lemon juice.
1 tablespoon fresh parsley chopped.
Salt & pepper to taste.
4 ounces uncooked pasta (I used spaghetti)

Tuna pasta is a delicious and easy-to-make recipe for kids. It's perfect for busy weeknights when you don't have much time to cook. To make this delicious dish, start by heating the olive oil in a large skillet over medium heat. Add the garlic and sauté until fragrant, about 1 minute. Add the tuna and stir to combine. Then add the lemon juice and parsley, season with salt and pepper to taste, and cook for another minute or two. Finally, add the uncooked pasta to the skillet and mix everything together. Cook according to directions on the box until al dente. Serve hot and enjoy! Tuna pasta is a delicious and nutritious meal that your kids will love. Enjoy!

Honey Soy Grilled Pork Chops

Ingredients:

4 pork chops
1/4 cup honey
1/4 cup soy sauce
2 tablespoons vegetable oil
2 cloves garlic, minced
1/2 teaspoon ground ginger
Salt and pepper

Instructions:

Preheat your grill to medium-high heat.
In a small bowl, whisk together the honey, soy sauce, vegetable oil, garlic, and ground ginger to make the marinade.
Season the pork chops with salt and pepper on both sides.
Place the pork chops in a shallow dish or large resealable bag and pour the marinade over them. Make sure the pork chops are fully coated in the marinade.
Cover the dish or seal the bag and refrigerate for at least 30 minutes or up to 4 hours to allow the pork chops to marinate.
Remove the pork chops from the marinade and discard any excess marinade.
Place the pork chops on the grill and cook for 5-6 minutes on each side or until they reach an internal temperature of 145°F.
Let the pork chops rest for a few minutes before serving to allow the juices to redistribute.
Serve the pork chops with your favorite side dishes and enjoy!
Note: You can also baste the pork chops with the leftover marinade while grilling for added flavor.

Easy Chicken Parm

Ingredients:

4 boneless, skinless chicken breasts
1 cup Italian seasoned breadcrumbs
1/2 cup grated Parmesan cheese
1 egg, beaten
1 cup marinara sauce
1 cup shredded mozzarella cheese
Salt and pepper
Olive oil
Fresh basil leaves, chopped

Instructions:

Preheat the oven to 375°F (190°C).
Season the chicken breasts with salt and pepper on both sides.
In a shallow dish, mix together the breadcrumbs and Parmesan cheese.
In another shallow dish, beat the egg.
Dip each chicken breast in the egg mixture, then coat it in the breadcrumb mixture.
Heat a few tablespoons of olive oil in a large skillet over medium heat.
Add the chicken breasts and cook for about 3-4 minutes on each side until golden brown.
Transfer the chicken breasts to a baking dish.
Spoon the marinara sauce over the chicken breasts.
Sprinkle the shredded mozzarella cheese on top.
Bake the chicken for 20-25 minutes or until the cheese is melted and bubbly.
Garnish with chopped fresh basil leaves and serve. Enjoy your easy chicken Parmesan!

Mahi Mahi Tacos

Ingredients:

1 lb. Mahi Mahi fillets, cut into small pieces
2 tablespoons olive oil
1 tablespoon chili powder
1/2 teaspoon garlic powder
1/2 teaspoon cumin
1/2 teaspoon smoked paprika
Salt and pepper
8 corn tortillas
1 avocado, sliced
1/2 red onion, sliced

For the slaw:

2 cups thinly sliced cabbage
1/2 cup thinly sliced red onion
1/4 cup chopped fresh cilantro
2 tablespoons lime juice
1 tablespoon olive oil
Salt and pepper

Instructions:

Preheat a skillet over medium-high heat.
In a small bowl, mix together the olive oil, chili powder, garlic powder, cumin, smoked paprika, salt, and pepper.
Add the Mahi Mahi pieces to the skillet and pour the spice mixture over them. Cook for 5-7 minutes or until the fish is cooked through, stirring occasionally.
While the fish is cooking, make the slaw by combining the cabbage, red onion, cilantro, lime juice, olive oil, salt, and pepper in a bowl. Mix well and set aside.
Heat the corn tortillas in a separate skillet or on the grill until they are warm and slightly charred.
To assemble the tacos, place some of the Mahi Mahi on each tortilla followed by some of the slaw, avocado slices, red onion slices, and chopped cilantro.
Squeeze some lime juice over the top of each taco and serve immediately.
Enjoy your delicious Mahi Mahi tacos!

Creamy Tomato Soup

Tomato Soup is a great lunch choice for kids because it's easy to make and packed with healthy ingredients. Plus, they will love the bright and vibrant colour! Here's what you'll need to make this delicious tomato soup recipe:

- 1-1.25kg/2lb 4oz-2lb 12oz ripe tomatoes

- 1 medium onion

- 1 small carrot

- 1 celery stick

- 2 tbsp olive oil

- 2 squirts of tomato purée (about 2 tsp)

- A good pinch of sugar

- 2 bay leaves

Once you've gathered all the ingredients, it's time to start cooking! Begin by heating the olive oil in a large saucepan and adding the diced onion, carrot, celery stick. Cook over medium heat for about 5 minutes until softened. Then add the tomatoes, purée, bay leaves and sugar. Cover with a lid and cook for 40 minutes. Once the soup is cooked, remove the bay leaves and blend until smooth with a blender.

Serve up this delicious tomato soup with some crusty bread or croutons on top and you have an easy, healthy lunch that your kids will love! Enjoy!

BBQ Tempeh Sandwiches

Ingredients:

1 package of tempeh, sliced into thin strips
1/2 cup of your favorite BBQ sauce
2 tablespoons apple cider vinegar
1 tablespoon olive oil
1/2 teaspoon garlic powder
1/2 teaspoon onion powder
Salt and pepper
4 hamburger buns
Sliced red onion (optional)
Sliced pickles (optional)
Coleslaw (optional)

Instructions:

Preheat a skillet over medium-high heat.
In a small bowl, whisk together the BBQ sauce, apple cider vinegar, olive oil, garlic powder, onion powder, salt, and pepper.
Add the sliced tempeh to the skillet and pour the BBQ sauce mixture over the top. Stir to coat the tempeh.
Cook the tempeh for 5-7 minutes or until it is crispy and golden brown, stirring occasionally.
While the tempeh is cooking, toast the hamburger buns on a separate skillet or on the grill.
To assemble the sandwiches, place some of the BBQ tempeh on the bottom half of each bun. Add some sliced red onion, pickles, and coleslaw if desired.
Top with the other half of the bun and serve immediately.
Enjoy your delicious BBQ tempeh sandwiches!

Chipotle Tofu & Pineapple Skewers

Ingredients:

1 block of firm tofu, drained and cut into 1-inch cubes
1/2 a fresh pineapple, cut into 1-inch cubes
1 red onion, cut into 1-inch cubes
2 tablespoons of olive oil
1 tablespoon of adobo sauce (from canned chipotle peppers)
1 teaspoon of honey
1 teaspoon of smoked paprika
1/2 teaspoon of garlic powder
Salt and black pepper, to taste
8-10 skewers (if using wooden skewers, soak them in water for at least 30 minutes before grilling)

Instructions:
In a small bowl, whisk together olive oil, adobo sauce, honey, smoked paprika, garlic powder, salt, and black pepper.
Thread the tofu, pineapple, and onion onto the skewers, alternating between them.
Brush the skewers with the chipotle marinade, making sure to coat them evenly.
Preheat your grill to medium-high heat. Once the grill is hot, place the skewers on the grill and cook for about 10-12 minutes, turning occasionally, until the tofu and pineapple are lightly charred and cooked through.
Once the skewers are cooked, remove them from the grill and place them on a serving dish. Serve the skewers hot and enjoy!
Note: If you don't have access to fresh pineapple, you can use canned pineapple chunks instead. Just make sure to drain them well before using.

Summer Panzanella

Ingredients:

1 small baguette, cut into bite-sized cubes
3 tablespoons olive oil, divided
Salt and black pepper, to taste
1 pint cherry tomatoes, halved
1 large cucumber, diced
1/2 red onion, thinly sliced
1/2 cup fresh basil leaves, torn into pieces
1/2 cup fresh mozzarella balls, halved
2 tablespoons red wine vinegar
1 garlic clove, minced

Instructions:

Preheat your oven to 375°F (190°C).
Toss the cubed bread with 2 tablespoons of olive oil, salt, and black pepper. Spread the bread cubes in a single layer on a baking sheet and bake for about 10-12 minutes, or until the bread is lightly toasted and crispy.
While the bread is toasting, prepare the other ingredients. In a large bowl, combine cherry tomatoes, cucumber, red onion, torn basil leaves, and fresh mozzarella.
In a small bowl, whisk together red wine vinegar, minced garlic, remaining 1 tablespoon of olive oil, salt, and black pepper.
Once the bread cubes are toasted, add them to the bowl with the other ingredients. Pour the dressing over the top and toss everything together until well combined.
Let the salad sit for about 15-20 minutes before serving, to allow the flavors to meld together.
Serve the Summer Panzanella salad as a main dish or as a side dish with your favorite grilled protein, and enjoy!
Note: You can customize this recipe by adding or substituting other vegetables or herbs, such as bell peppers, olives, or parsley, depending on your taste preferences.

Mushroom Burger

Here's a recipe for a delicious mushroom burger:

Ingredients:

4 portobello mushroom caps
1/4 cup balsamic vinegar
2 tablespoons olive oil
1 teaspoon dried thyme
1/2 teaspoon garlic powder
Salt and black pepper
4 burger buns
Toppings of your choice
(lettuce, tomato, onion, etc.)

Instructions:

Preheat your grill or grill pan to medium-high heat.
Clean the portobello mushrooms and remove the stems. Use a spoon to gently scrape out the gills and discard them.
In a small bowl, whisk together the balsamic vinegar, olive oil, thyme, garlic powder, salt, and pepper.
Brush the marinade over both sides of the mushroom caps, making sure they are fully coated.
Place the mushrooms on the grill and cook for 4-5 minutes on each side, or until they are tender and juicy.
While the mushrooms are cooking, toast your burger buns on the grill.
Assemble your burgers by placing the cooked mushrooms on the toasted buns and adding your desired toppings.
Serve immediately and enjoy your delicious mushroom burger!

Sweet Potato Salad

Ingredients:

2 large sweet potatoes, peeled and cubed
1/2 red onion, diced
1 red bell pepper, diced
1/4 cup chopped fresh cilantro
1/4 cup chopped pecans
2 tablespoons olive oil
2 tablespoons apple cider vinegar
1 tablespoon honey
1 teaspoon Dijon mustard
Salt and black pepper, to taste

Instructions:

Preheat oven to 400°F (200°C).
Spread the sweet potato cubes in a single layer on a baking sheet lined with parchment paper. Drizzle with 1 tablespoon of olive oil and sprinkle with salt and pepper. Toss to coat.
Roast sweet potatoes for 25-30 minutes or until they are tender and golden brown. Remove from the oven and let cool.
In a small bowl, whisk together 1 tablespoon of olive oil, apple cider vinegar, honey, Dijon mustard, salt, and pepper until well combined.
In a large mixing bowl, combine the cooled sweet potatoes, diced red onion, diced red bell pepper, chopped cilantro, and chopped pecans.
Pour the dressing over the sweet potato mixture and toss to coat.
Serve chilled or at room temperature.

This sweet potato salad is perfect for a healthy and flavorful side dish for any meal. Enjoy!

Easy Vegan Noodle

Ingredients:

8 oz of noodles of your choice (such as spaghetti or udon)
1/2 cup chopped mushrooms
1/2 cup chopped carrots
1/2 cup chopped red bell pepper
1/2 cup chopped green onions
2 cloves garlic, minced
1/4 cup soy sauce
1 tablespoon sesame oil
1 tablespoon rice vinegar
1 tablespoon maple syrup
1 teaspoon ginger paste
1 teaspoon cornstarch
Salt and black pepper, to taste

Instructions:

Cook the noodles according to the package instructions. Drain and set aside.
In a small bowl, whisk together the soy sauce, sesame oil, rice vinegar, maple syrup, ginger paste, cornstarch, salt, and pepper.
In a large skillet, heat some oil over medium-high heat. Add the chopped mushrooms, carrots, and red bell pepper. Cook for 5-7 minutes or until the vegetables are tender.
Add the minced garlic and cook for an additional minute, stirring constantly.
Add the chopped green onions and the soy sauce mixture to the skillet. Cook for 2-3 minutes or until the sauce thickens.
Add the cooked noodles to the skillet and toss to coat with the sauce. Serve hot and enjoy!

This vegan noodle dish is quick and easy to make, and it's packed with flavor and nutrients. You can customize the recipe by using your favorite type of noodles and vegetables. It's a great option for a weeknight dinner or a quick lunch.

Creamy Salmon Pasta

Ingredients
2 salmon fillets.
1 tbsp olive oil, plus 1 tsp if roasting.
175g penne.
2 shallots or 1 small onion, finely chopped.
1 garlic clove, crushed.
100ml white wine.
200ml double cream or crème fraîche.
¼ lemon, zested and juiced.

Creamy salmon pasta is a delicious and easy recipe for kids. This delicious meal can be prepared in just a few simple steps.

To begin, preheat your oven to 200°c (gas mark 6) and brush the salmon fillets with 1 tbsp of olive oil. Place them in the oven to bake for 12-15 minutes until cooked through. Once the salmon is cooked, flake it into small pieces and set aside.

Bring a large pot of salted water to the boil and cook your penne according to packet instructions until al dente.

Meanwhile, heat 1 tsp of olive oil in a large skillet over medium-high heat. Add the shallots or onions and garlic to the skillet and sauté for a few minutes until softened. Add the white wine, cream or crème fraîche, lemon zest, lemon juice and flaked salmon pieces. Simmer gently over low heat for around 5-7 minutes until the sauce has thickened slightly.

To serve, drain the cooked penne and combine with the sauce. Divide into plates and enjoy your delicious creamy salmon pasta!

This delicious recipe is sure to be a hit with all the family - even picky eaters will love it! With only a few simple ingredients, this meal can be prepared in no time at all so why not give it a try tonight? Enjoy!

Grilled Baked Potatoes

Ingredients:

4 large potatoes (russet or Idaho)
2 tablespoons olive oil
1 teaspoon salt
1/2 teaspoon black pepper
1/4 cup grated Parmesan cheese
2 tablespoons chopped fresh parsley
2 tablespoons chopped fresh chives
2 garlic cloves, minced

Instructions:

Preheat the grill to medium-high heat.
Wash the potatoes thoroughly and pat them dry with a paper towel.
Cut each potato into thick slices (about 1/2 inch thick).
In a large bowl, mix together the olive oil, salt, black pepper, Parmesan cheese, parsley, chives, and minced garlic.
Add the potato slices to the bowl and toss until they are well coated with the oil mixture.
Place the potato slices on the grill and cook for 5-7 minutes per side, or until they are golden brown and tender when pierced with a fork.
Remove the potatoes from the grill and let them cool for a few minutes before serving.
Serve the grilled baked potatoes as a side dish or appetizer. They pair well with grilled meats or vegetables.
Enjoy your delicious Grilled Baked Potatoes!

Sesame Chicken Meatballs

Ingredients

1 pound ground chicken.
½ cup breadcrumbs.
2 tablespoons soy sauce.
1 tablespoon Shaoxing wine (or mirin)
½ tablespoon sesame oil.
1 tablespoon ginger, freshly grated.
½ teaspoon garlic powder.
2 tablespoons green onions, finely chopped.

These chicken sesame meatballs are a healthy and easy dinner option that your kids will love. To prepare the meatballs, simply combine all of the ingredients in a large bowl and mix together until everything is well-incorporated. Once the mixture is ready, form it into small balls with your hands. Place them on a parchment paper-lined baking sheet, and bake at 350°F for about 20 minutes or until the meatballs are cooked through. Serve hot with a side of your favorite vegetables or salad. Enjoy!

This is an easy recipe that requires minimal preparation time, making it perfect for busy weeknights. Plus, you can use leftover meatballs as a quick and simple lunch the next day. So when you're looking for a healthy dinner option that your kids will love, give these chicken sesame meatballs a try!

Grilled Cod Tacos with Chipotle Crema

Ingredients:

1 lb. cod fillets
2 tbsp. olive oil
1 tbsp. chili powder
1 tsp. cumin
1/2 tsp. garlic powder
Salt and pepper
8 corn tortillas
1 cup shredded cabbage
1 avocado, sliced
1 lime, cut into wedges

For the chipotle crema:

1/2 cup sour cream
1 tbsp. adobo sauce (from a can of chipotle peppers)
Juice of 1/2 lime
Salt to taste

Instructions:

Preheat grill to medium-high heat.
In a small bowl, mix together olive oil, chili powder, cumin, garlic powder, salt, and pepper. Brush both sides of the cod fillets with the spice mixture.
Grill the cod for about 3-4 minutes per side, or until cooked through.
While the cod is grilling, make the chipotle crema. In a small bowl, mix together sour cream, adobo sauce, lime juice, and salt. Adjust seasoning to taste.
Warm the corn tortillas on the grill or in a skillet.
Assemble the tacos by placing some shredded cabbage on each tortilla, followed by a piece of grilled cod, sliced avocado, and a dollop of chipotle crema. Serve with lime wedges on the side.
Enjoy your delicious Grilled Cod Tacos with Chipotle Crema!

Spinach And Feta Pie

INGREDIENTS
400 G (14 OZ) SPINACH LEAVES, FRESH OR FROZEN.
FRESH NUTMEG.
SEA SALT AND FRESHLY GROUND PEPPER.
200 G (7 OZ) FETA.
SQUEEZE OF LEMON JUICE.
3-4 LARGE SHEETS OF READY-ROLLED PUFF PASTRY (PREFERABLY MADE WITH BUTTER)
1 EGG BEATEN WITH A DASH OF MILK FOR THE EGG WASH.

Spinach and feta pie is a healthy, low-budget recipe that is easy and fast to make. This savory dish consists of 400 grams (14 oz) of fresh or frozen spinach leaves, fresh nutmeg, sea salt, freshly ground pepper, 200 grams (7 oz) of feta cheese and a squeeze of lemon juice. To top it off, you'll need 3-4 large sheets of ready-rolled puff pastry (preferably made with butter). Once the ingredients are prepared, simply assemble and brush your pie with an egg wash beaten with a dash of milk. Then bake for 25 minutes or until golden brown in a preheated oven. You can serve this healthy and delicious pie as an appetizer, side dish or even main course. Enjoy!

Vegetarian Lasagna

Vegetarian lasagna makes a delicious, kid-friendly meal. It's easy to make and packed with nutrition from vegetables like carrots, bell peppers, zucchini, and onion. To get started on this delicious recipe, you'll need the following ingredients: 2 tablespoons extra-virgin olive oil, 3 large carrots (chopped into about 1 cup), 1 red bell pepper (chopped), 1 medium zucchini (chopped), 1 medium yellow onion (chopped), ¼ teaspoon salt, and 5 to 6 ounces of baby spinach.

To begin cooking your vegetarian lasagna, heat the olive oil in a skillet over medium-high heat. Add the carrots, bell pepper, zucchini, onion, and salt. Cook the vegetables until they are soft and tender, stirring occasionally. Then, add the spinach and cook for a few minutes longer until it wilts.

Once your vegetables are cooked through, you are ready to assemble your delicious vegetarian lasagna! Layer a baking dish with pre-cooked lasagna noodles, followed by the cooked vegetable mixture and then some delicious sauce. Top with shredded cheese and bake in an oven preheated to 350 degrees for 30 minutes. Your delicious vegetarian lasagna is now ready to enjoy - a perfect meal that kids will love!

Making vegetarian meals doesn't have to be difficult. With delicious recipes like this vegetarian lasagna, you can easily create delicious and nutritious meals that the whole family will enjoy. Give it a try today!

Vegan Burritos

Ingredients:

1 cup (185 g) of uncooked brown rice
1 can (15 oz/425 g) of black beans, drained and rinsed
1 red bell pepper, diced
1/2 red onion, diced
1 avocado, diced
1 jalapeño pepper, diced (optional)
1 tbsp (15 ml) of olive oil
1 tsp (5 g) of ground cumin
1/2 tsp (2.5 g) of garlic powder
Salt and pepper, to taste
4-6 large flour tortillas
Vegan shredded cheese (such as cheddar or mozzarella) (optional)
Salsa, guacamole, or vegan sour cream, for serving (optional)

Instructions:

Cook the brown rice according to the package instructions.
In a mixing bowl, combine the black beans, red bell pepper, red onion, avocado, jalapeño pepper (if using), olive oil, cumin, garlic powder, salt, and pepper. Stir well to combine.
Heat a large skillet over medium heat. Add the black bean mixture to the skillet and cook for 5-7 minutes, stirring occasionally, until the vegetables are tender and the beans are heated through.
Warm the flour tortillas in the microwave or oven.
To assemble the vegan burritos, place a spoonful of brown rice in the center of each tortilla, followed by a spoonful of the black bean mixture. If using, sprinkle vegan shredded cheese on top.
Fold the sides of the tortilla over the filling, then roll it up tightly. Repeat with the remaining tortillas and filling.
Serve the vegan burritos with salsa, guacamole, or vegan sour cream, if desired.
Enjoy your delicious and filling vegan burritos for lunch or dinner! You can also customize them by adding your favorite vegetables or toppings.

Pasta Alla Gricia

Ingredients:

1 pound bucatini or spaghetti
6 ounces pancetta, diced
1/2 cup grated Pecorino Romano cheese
1/2 cup grated Parmesan cheese
1/2 teaspoon black pepper
2 tablespoons extra-virgin olive oil
Salt to taste

Instructions:

Bring a large pot of salted water to a boil. Add the pasta and cook until al dente.
While the pasta is cooking, heat the olive oil in a large skillet over medium heat. Add the pancetta and cook until it's crispy, about 8 minutes.
Once the pasta is cooked, reserve 1 cup of the pasta cooking water and drain the pasta.
Add the drained pasta to the skillet with the pancetta. Toss to coat the pasta in the pancetta fat.
Add the reserved pasta water to the skillet and stir to combine.
Remove the skillet from the heat and add the grated Pecorino Romano cheese, Parmesan cheese, and black pepper. Toss everything together until the cheese is melted and the pasta is coated in the sauce.
Taste and adjust seasoning as needed, adding salt if necessary.
Serve hot, garnished with additional grated cheese and black pepper if desired.
Enjoy your delicious Pasta alla Gricia!

Pasta Al Limone

Ingredients:

1 lb (450 g) spaghetti or linguine
1 cup (240 ml) heavy cream
1/2 cup (120 ml) freshly squeezed lemon juice (about 2-3 lemons)
1 tbsp (15 ml) lemon zest
1/2 cup (120 ml) grated Parmesan cheese
1/4 cup (60 ml) unsalted butter
Salt and pepper, to taste
Fresh parsley, chopped (optional)

Instructions:
Bring a large pot of salted water t a boil. Add the pasta and cook according to package instructions until al dente. Drain and set aside.
In a large saucepan, melt the butter over medium heat. Add the heavy cream, lemon juice, and lemon zest, and stir to combine.
Cook for 2-3 minutes, until slightly thickened.
Add the Parmesan cheese to the sauce and stir until melted and smooth.
Add the cooked pasta to the sauce and toss to coat. If the sauce is too thick, add a bit of the reserved pasta water to thin it out.
Season with salt and pepper to taste. Serve hot, garnished with chopped parsley if desired.
Enjoy your delicious Pasta al Limone!

Chicken Pot Pie

INGREDIENTS

1 POUND SKINLESS, BONELESS CHICKEN BREAST HALVES - CUBED.
1 CUP SLICED CARROTS.
1 CUP FROZEN GREEN PEAS.
½ CUP SLICED CELERY.
⅓ CUP BUTTER.
⅓ CUP CHOPPED ONION.
⅓ CUP ALL-PURPOSE FLOUR.
½ TEASPOON SALT.
GREAT VALUE IODIZED SALT, 26 OZ.

Chicken pot pie is an easy and fast recipe that is perfect for busy weeknights. It's a comforting dish filled with cubed chicken, carrots, peas, celery, butter, onion and all-purpose flour that can be prepared in no time. To make this easy chicken recipe even tastier, you can add ½ teaspoon of salt for seasoning.

If you are looking for easy and fast chicken recipes, then this is the one for you. All you have to do is cube the chicken breasts, slice the carrots and celery, gather all other ingredients and mix them together in a large bowl until everything is well combined. Then transfer the mixture into an oven-safe dish and bake for about 30 minutes or until golden brown. Enjoy your easy and delicious chicken pot pie!

That's all there is to making this easy chicken pot pie recipe. With just a few easy steps, you can prepare a comforting and delicious meal in no time. So if you're looking for easy and fast chicken recipes to make for dinner, then this easy chicken pot pie should be your go-to dish.

The key to making the perfect chicken pot pie is to use all the ingredients listed above and season it with Great Value Iodized Salt for added flavor. With just a few easy steps, you can have a delicious meal that's ready in no time! So, next time you're looking for easy and fast chicken recipes, give this easy chicken pot pie a try. Enjoy!

Chicken Quesadillas

Ingredients

1 pound skinless, boneless chicken breast, diced.
1 (1.27 ounce) packet fajita seasoning.
1 tablespoon vegetable oil.
2 green bell peppers, chopped.
2 red bell peppers, chopped.
1 onion, chopped. ...
10 (10 inch) flour tortillas.
1 (8 ounce) package shredded Cheddar cheese.

Chicken quesadillas make for a healthy and easy dinner for the whole family. To start preparing, dice the boneless chicken breasts and season with fajita seasoning. In a large skillet over medium heat, heat vegetable oil and add in the diced chicken breast, green bell peppers, red bell peppers, and onions. Cook until vegetables are softened and chicken is cooked through. To assemble the quesadillas, place about ¼ cup of cheese onto one side of a tortilla. Top with cooked vegetables and chicken, then add another ¼ cup of cheese to the top. Fold over into a half-moon shape and cook in a skillet on medium-high heat until golden brown. Repeat this process with the remaining tortillas. Serve warm and enjoy!

For a fun variation, try adding black beans to the quesadillas or swapping out Cheddar cheese for Monterey Jack. Using flavorful ingredients like jalapenos, salsa, and guacamole can also liven up this classic dish. Chicken quesadillas make for a healthy and delicious dinner that can be customized to fit the tastes of any family. Enjoy!

Chicken Caesar Salad

If you want to make an easy and fast chicken caesar salad, then you've come to the right place! This recipe is easy to prepare, and uses simple ingredients that are easy to find. To start, chop 6 cups of tightly packed romaine lettuce and set aside. Next cook 1 pound of boneless skinless chicken breasts until cooked through, then cut into strips. In a bowl, mix together the chicken strips, lettuce and ½ cup of finely shredded parmesan cheese. Add in ½ cup of seasoned croutons and ¼ cup of creamy caesar dressing. Mix everything together and serve your easy and delicious chicken caesar salad! For more easy-to-make chicken recipes, check out our website for more ideas. Enjoy!

Grilled Bruschetta Chicken

Ingredients:

4 boneless, skinless chicken breasts
2 tablespoons olive oil
1 teaspoon dried basil
1 teaspoon dried oregano
1/2 teaspoon garlic powder
Salt and pepper
1 large tomato, diced
2 cloves garlic, minced
1/4 cup chopped fresh basil
1 tablespoon balsamic vinegar
1 tablespoon olive oil
Salt and pepper
4 slices of Italian bread
1/4 cup shredded Parmesan cheese

Instructions:

Preheat your grill to medium-high heat.
In a small bowl, whisk together 2 tablespoons of olive oil, dried basil, dried oregano, garlic powder, salt, and pepper. Rub the mixture all over the chicken breasts.
In another small bowl, combine the diced tomato, minced garlic, chopped fresh basil, balsamic vinegar, 1 tablespoon of olive oil, salt, and pepper. Stir to combine and set aside.
Grill the chicken breasts for 6-8 minutes per side, or until the internal temperature reaches 165°F.
While the chicken is cooking, brush the slices of Italian bread with olive oil and grill for 1-2 minutes per side, or until toasted.
Top each slice of grilled bread with a chicken breast, then spoon the tomato mixture over the chicken.
Sprinkle each chicken breast with shredded Parmesan cheese.
Serve hot and enjoy your delicious grilled bruschetta chicken!
Note: You can also add a drizzle of balsamic glaze over the top for an extra burst of flavor.

Honey Balsamic Grilled Chicken Thighs

Ingredients:

4 bone-in, skin-on chicken thighs
1/4 cup balsamic vinegar
2 tablespoons honey
2 tablespoons olive oil
1 tablespoon Dijon mustard
2 cloves garlic, minced
1/2 teaspoon dried oregano
Salt and pepper
Chopped fresh parsley, for garnish

Instructions:

In a small bowl, whisk together the balsamic vinegar, honey, olive oil, Dijon mustard, minced garlic, dried oregano, salt, and pepper.
Place the chicken thighs in a large resealable plastic bag and pour the marinade over them. Seal the bag and toss to coat the chicken evenly.
Refrigerate for at least 30 minutes, or up to 4 hours.
Preheat your grill to medium-high heat.
Remove the chicken from the marinade and discard any excess marinade.
Place the chicken on the grill, skin side down, and cook for 6-8 minutes per side, or until the internal temperature reaches 165°F and the skin is crispy and browned.
Brush the chicken with any remaining marinade during the last few minutes of grilling.
Remove the chicken from the grill and let it rest for a few minutes before serving.
Garnish with chopped fresh parsley before serving.
Enjoy your delicious honey balsamic grilled chicken thighs!

Pineapple Chicken Casserole

Here's a list of ingredients for a pineapple chicken casserole:

2 cups cubed cooked chicken
1 can (10-1/2 ounces) condensed cream of mushroom soup
1 cup pineapple tidbits
2 celery ribs, chopped
1 tablespoon chopped green onion
1 tablespoon reduced-sodium soy sauce
1 can (3 ounces) chow mein noodles, divided

Instructions:

Preheat the oven to 350°F (175°C).

In a large bowl, combine the chicken, cream of mushroom soup, pineapple tidbits, chopped celery, green onion, and soy sauce.

Pour the mixture into a 2-quart baking dish.

Crush half of the chow mein noodles and sprinkle them over the top of the chicken mixture.

Bake the casserole in the preheated oven for 30 minutes, or until heated through and the top is golden and crispy.

Serve the casserole hot, garnished with the remaining chow mein noodles and additional chopped green onion, if desired. Enjoy!

Ravioli Lasagna

This delicious ravioli lasagna recipe is sure to be a hit with kids and adults alike! To make this delicious dish, you will need 1 pound of ground beef, 1 jar (28 ounces) spaghetti sauce, 1 package (25 ounces) frozen sausage or cheese ravioli, 1-1/2 cups shredded part-skim mozzarella cheese and minced fresh basil (optional).

Begin by cooking the ground beef in a large skillet over medium-high heat until no longer pink, stirring occasionally. Drain off any fat. Add spaghetti sauce to the cooked beef and bring mixture to a boil. Reduce heat; simmer for about 10 minutes or until heated through, stirring occasionally.

Meanwhile, cook ravioli according to package directions. Drain and set aside. Preheat oven to 350°F (175°C). In a greased 13x9-inch baking dish, layer one-third of the beef mixture, half of the cooked ravioli, and one-third of the cheese. Repeat layers. Top with remaining beef mixture and cheese.

Bake, uncovered, for 25 to 30 minutes or until bubbly and cheese is melted. If desired, sprinkle with basil before serving. Enjoy! With a few simple ingredients, this delicious recipe makes an easy meal that the whole family will love! Try it today for a delicious meal that will keep the kids asking for more. Bon Appétit!

Bacon Mushroom Pasta

Ingredients

8 ounces uncooked pasta (I used bucatini)
6 strips bacon cut into small pieces.
7 ounces cremini mushrooms sliced.
2 cloves garlic minced.
1/3 cup chicken broth or dry white wine.
1/4 teaspoon Italian seasoning.
1 teaspoon lemon juice.
1 teaspoon flour.

If you're looking for delicious recipes that kids will love, this bacon mushroom pasta is the perfect choice. It's easy to make and packed with flavor. To start, cook 8 ounces of uncooked bucatini pasta according to package instructions. Once cooked, drain and set aside.

In a large skillet over medium-high heat, cook the bacon until crisp, about 5 minutes. Remove the bacon with a slotted spoon and set aside. To the same skillet, add 7 ounces of sliced cremini mushrooms and cook for 4-5 minutes or until softened.

Add 2 cloves of minced garlic to the skillet and sauté for an additional 30 seconds. Add in 1/3 cup of chicken broth or dry white wine and simmer for 2 minutes. Stir in 1/4 teaspoon of Italian seasoning, 1 teaspoon of lemon juice, and 1 teaspoon of flour.

Return the bacon to the skillet and add the cooked pasta. Continue cooking until the sauce has thickened, stirring occasionally. Serve hot with freshly grated Parmesan cheese.

This delicious bacon mushroom pasta is sure to be a hit with the kids, and it's simple enough for even beginner cooks to prepare. With a few simple ingredients and easy-to-follow instructions, you can have this delicious dish on the table in no time! Give this delicious recipe a try tonight! Enjoy

I want to take a moment to express my heartfelt gratitude for your recent purchase of my recipe book. As a passionate food lover, nothing makes me happier than sharing my favorite recipes with others. Your decision to invest in my book not only supports my dream, but also shows your commitment to expanding your culinary horizons.

I sincerely hope that the recipes in the book will inspire you to try new things and add some excitement to your meals.

Thank you again for your support and for being a part of this journey with me. I hope my book will bring you many happy and delicious moments in the kitchen.

www.ingramcontent.com/pod-product-compliance
Lightning Source LLC
Chambersburg PA
CBHW041152110526
44590CB00027B/4204